When Gran was a girl

CONTENTS

Now

When Gran was a girl

she helped her mum.

3

Gran helped with the shopping.

4

Frozen Food

I help with the shopping.

Then

Gran helped with the cooking.

I help with the cooking.

Gran helped with the washing.

I help with the washing.

Gran helped her mum.

10

I help my mum.

Then   Now

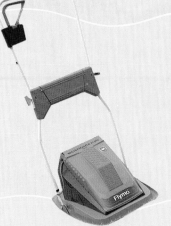